Now I Know

What is a Reptile

Written by Susan Kuchalla

Illustrated by Paul Harvey

Troll Associates

Library of Congress Cataloging in Publication Data

Kuchalla, Susan.
  What is a reptile.

  (Now I know)
  Summary: Simple text and illustrations introduce
some of the major characteristics of a variety
of reptiles.
  1. Reptiles—Juvenile literature. [1. Reptiles]
I. Harvey, Paul, 1926-   , ill. II. Title.
QL665.K82   597.9   81-11364
ISBN 0-89375-672-5   AACR2
ISBN 0-89375-673-3 (pbk.)

10   9   8   7   6   5   4   3   2   1

What is a reptile?

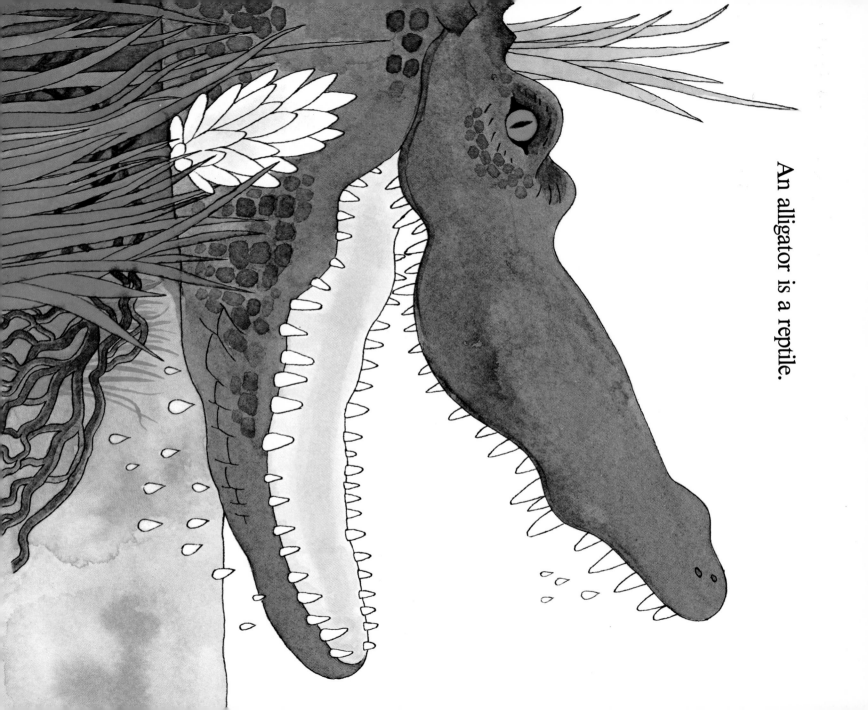

An alligator is a reptile.

A turtle is a reptile.

Snakes and lizards are reptiles.

And even dinosaurs were reptiles.

Reptiles are many sizes.

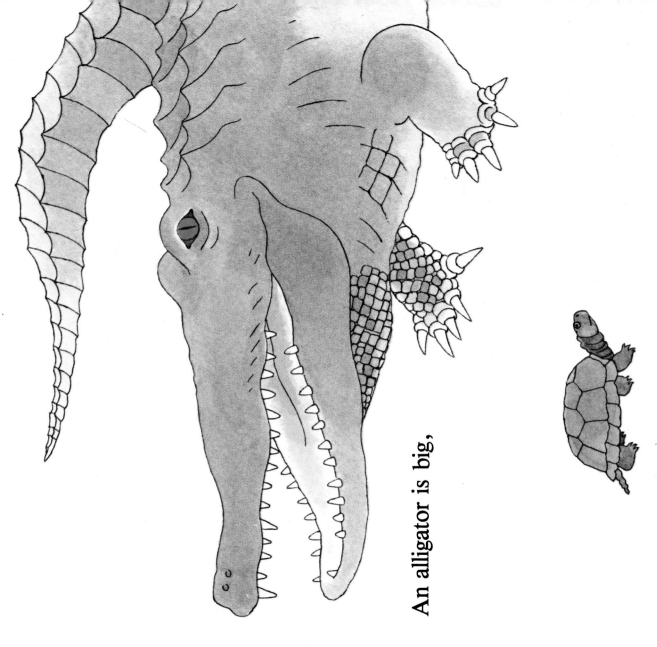

An alligator is big,

and a turtle is small.

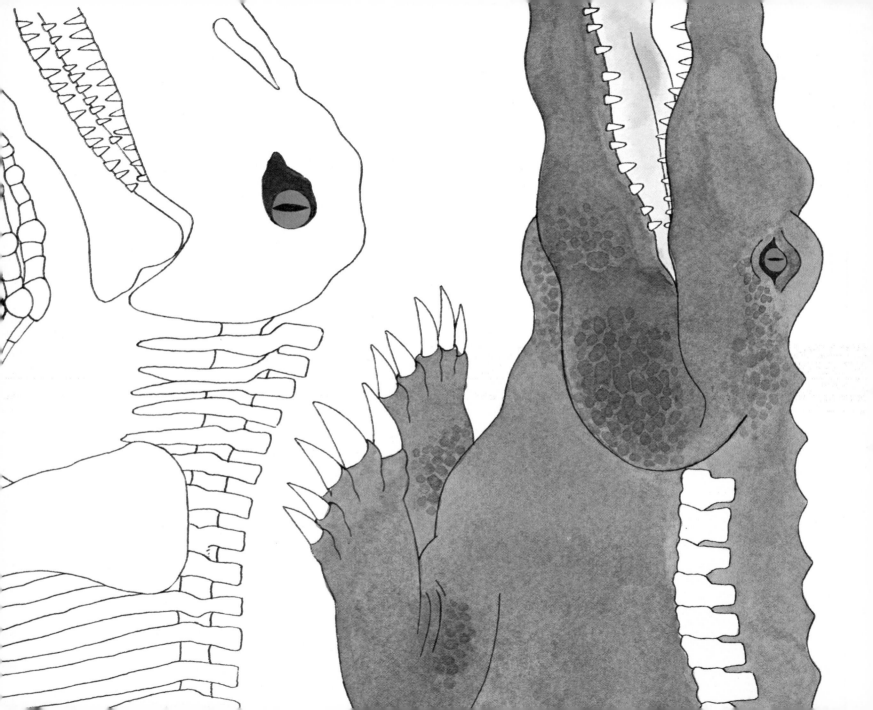

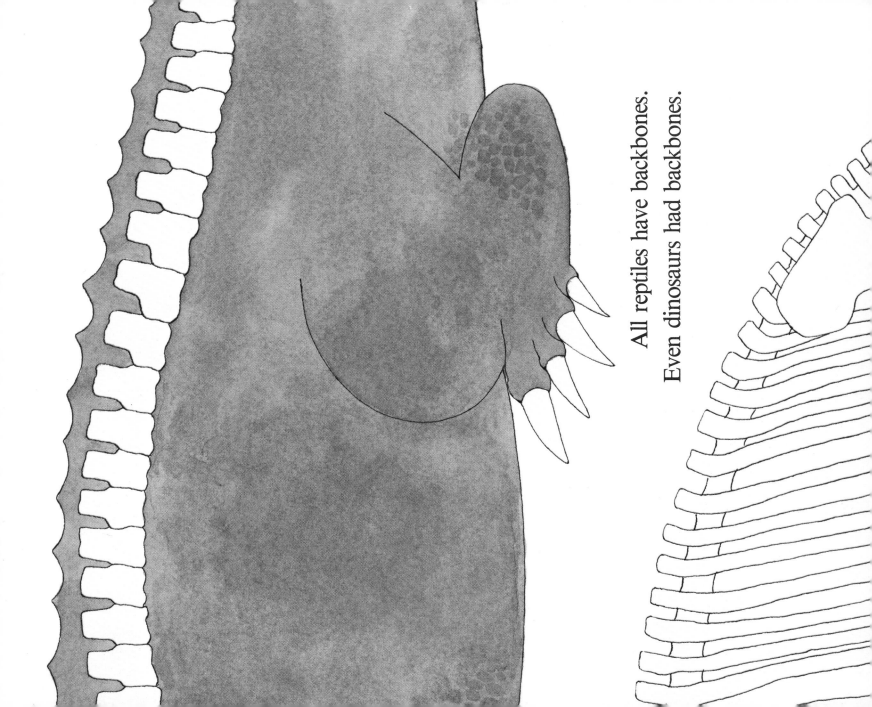

All reptiles have backbones.
Even dinosaurs had backbones.

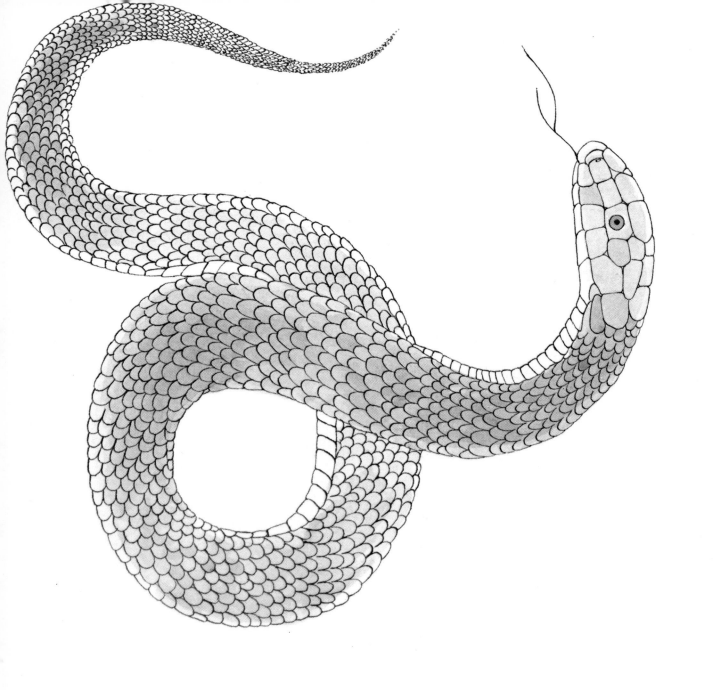

Most reptiles have skin covered with scales.

But a turtle has a shell.

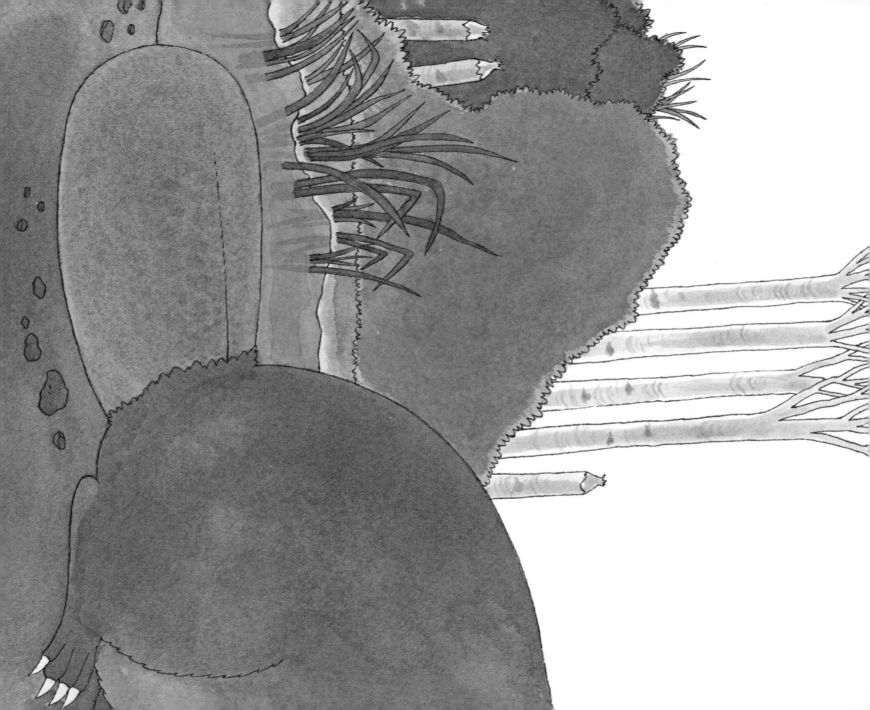

When a turtle is afraid . . . .
it pulls its arms and legs into the shell.
Then it closes the shell tightly.

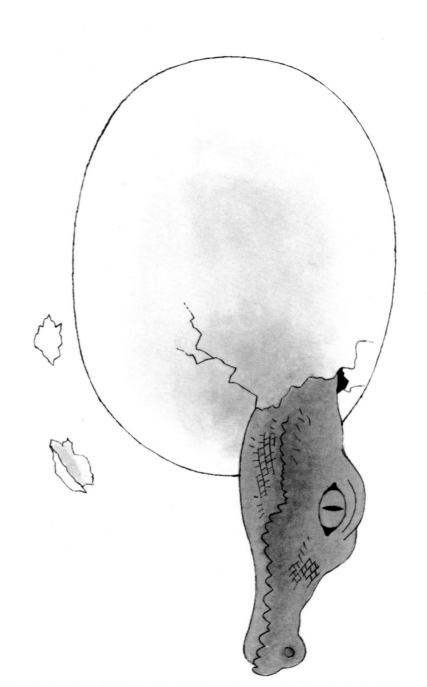

Most reptiles hatch from eggs.

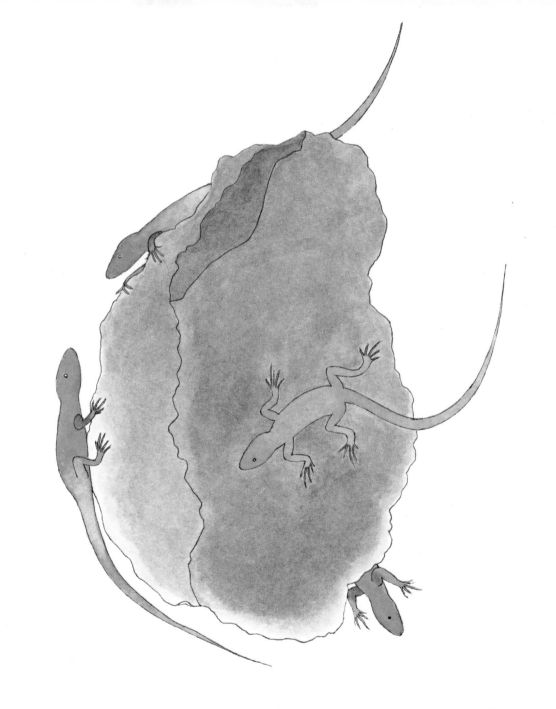

But some are born alive.

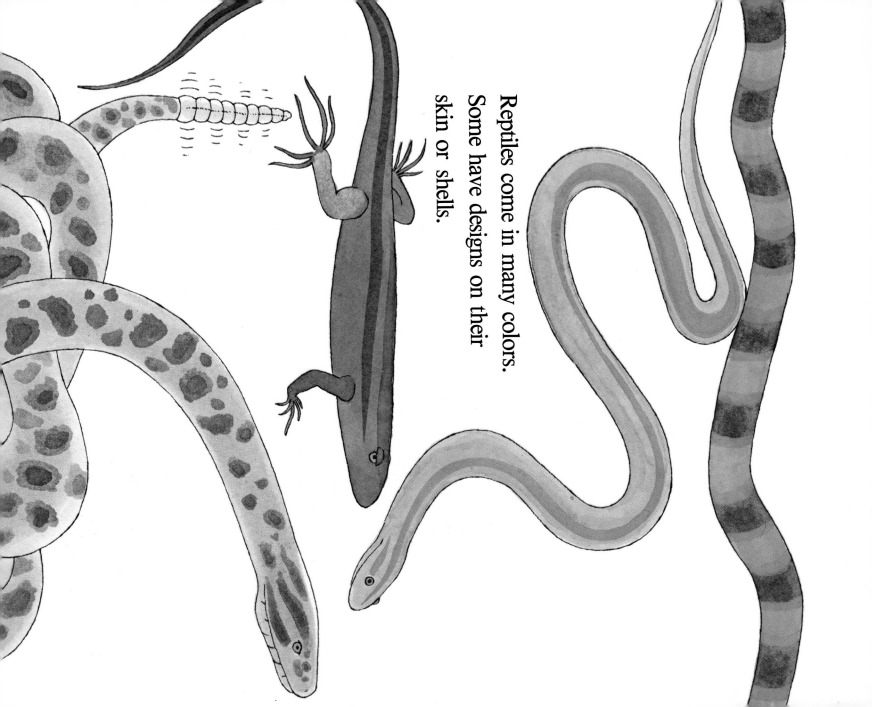

Reptiles come in many colors.
Some have designs on their
skin or shells.

Chameleons are lizards that can change their colors. Some chameleons are green when they are hiding.

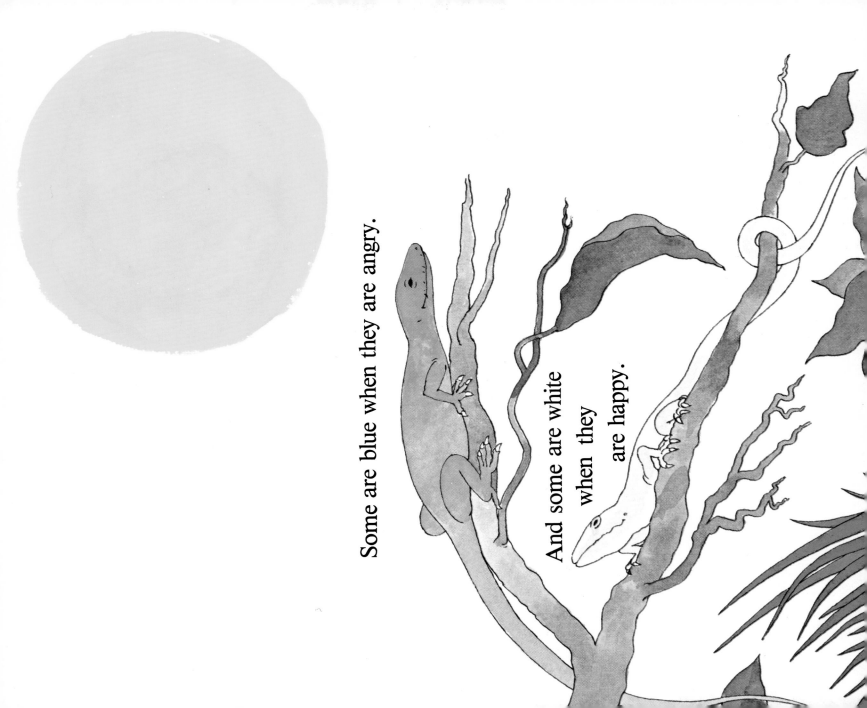

Some are blue when they are angry.

And some are white when they are happy.

Most reptile babies must take care of themselves.
Baby sea turtles never even know their mother!

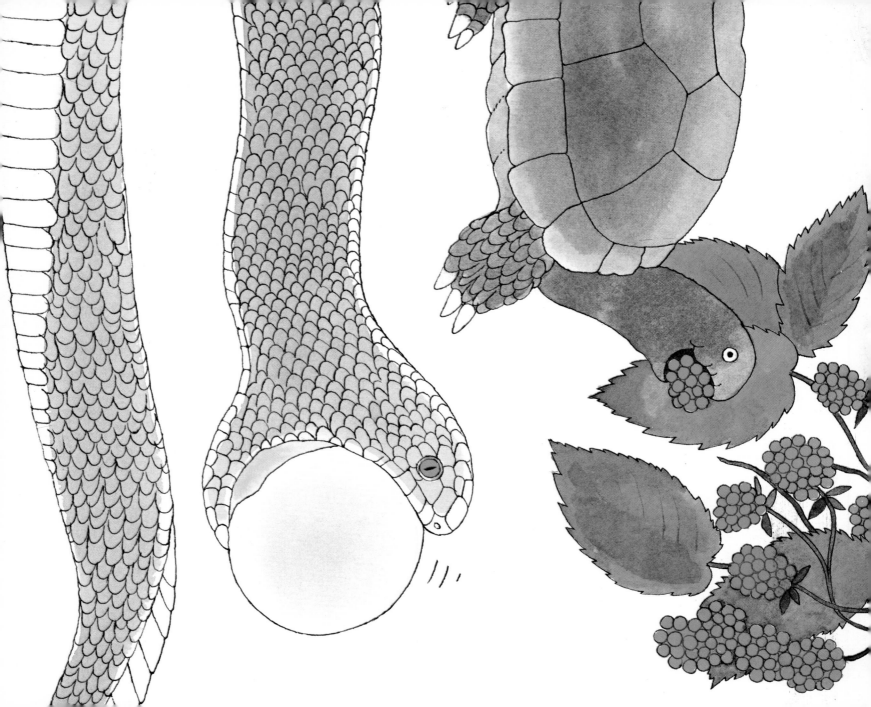

Some reptiles eat meat or fish.
Others eat plants or eggs.

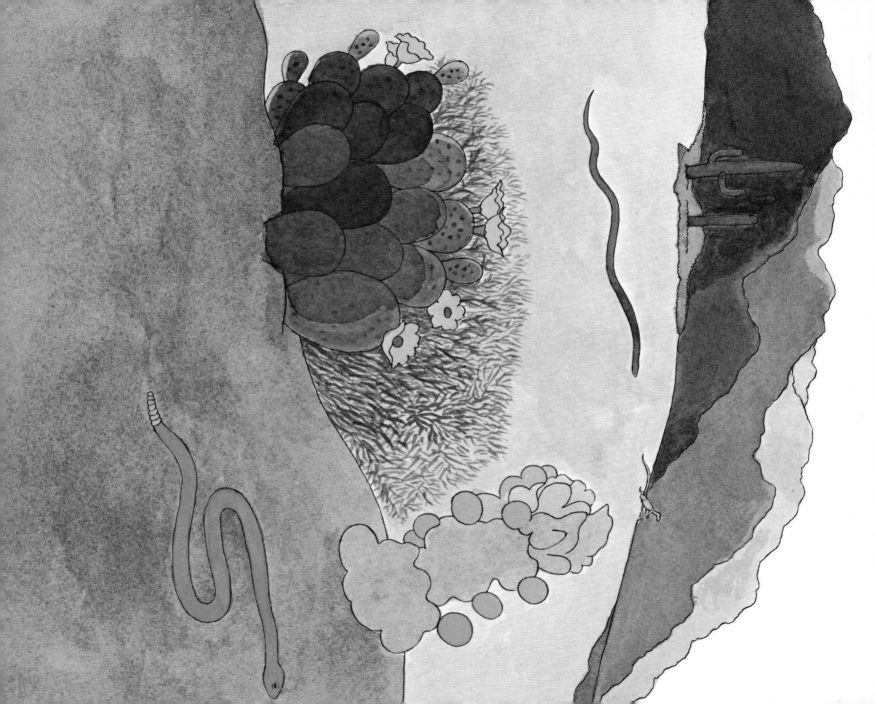

Reptiles live in many places.
Some live in hot, dry deserts.
Some live in oceans, lakes, and rivers.

And some live in warm, wet swamps.

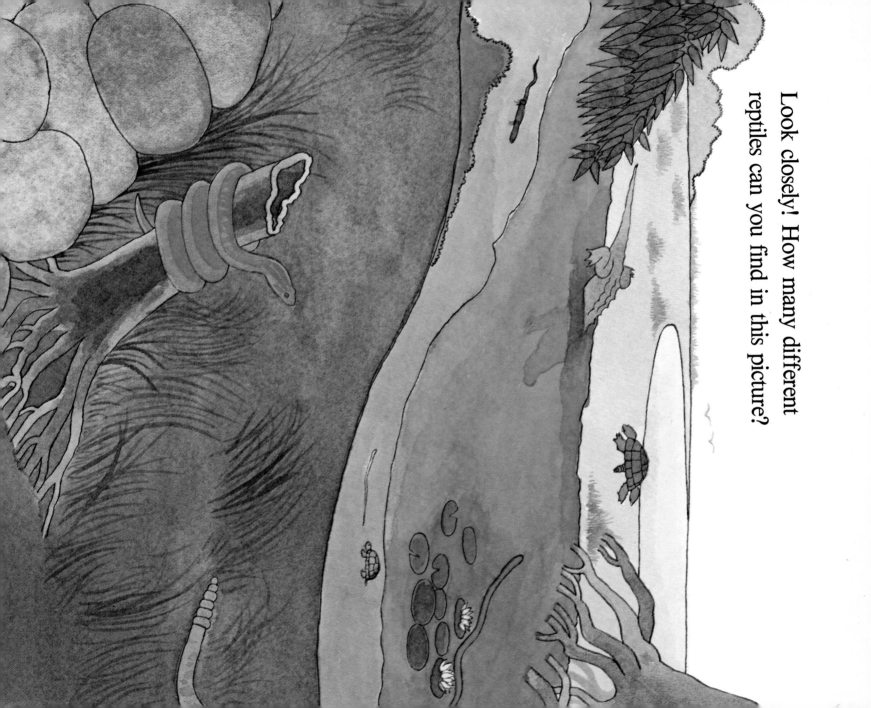

Look closely! How many different reptiles can you find in this picture?

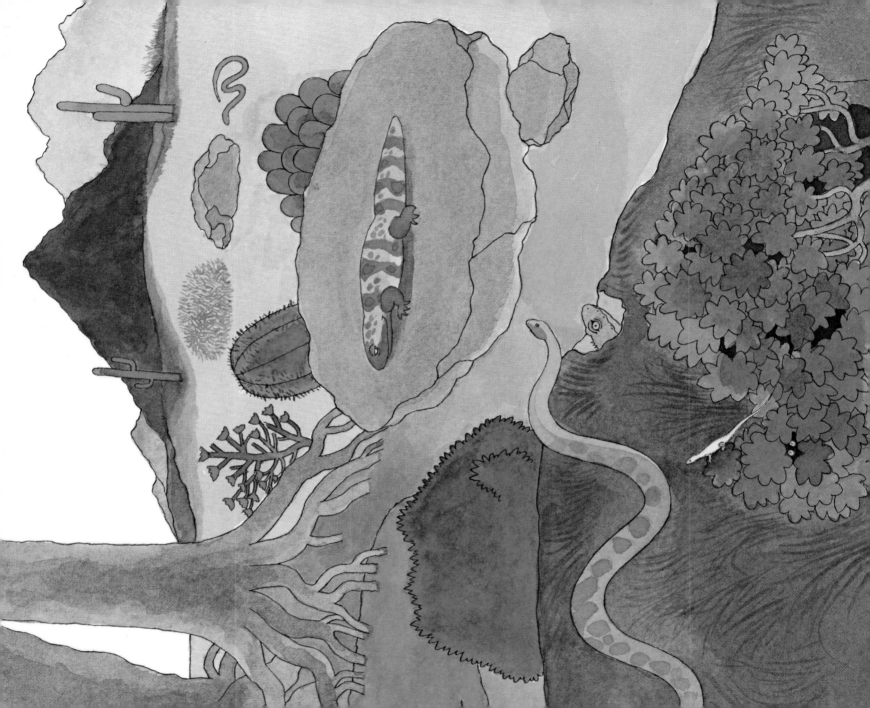